TWINS TO ONE

COPING STRATEGIES FOR A SINGLE PARENT
WITH TWINS

AUDREY MCLEAN

Twins to One Copyright © 2017 by Audrey McLean

All rights reserved. No part of this publication may be reproduced, distributed, or transmitted in any form, including photocopying, recording, or other electronic or mechanical methods without prior permission of the publisher.

First published in USA

ISBN: 9781973466116

DEDICATION

This book is dedicated to my beautiful twin daughters, Jules and Jayde.

ACKNOWLEDGEMENT

I would like to thank my two lovely, and brilliant sisters, Andrea and Novelette, for their input in my book.

ABOUT THE AUTHOR

Audrey McLean is a Neonatal Intensive Care Unit Registered Nurse with over fifteen years of experience. She has also been a Pharmaceutical Sales Representative for the last fourteen years.

She has a Bachelor of Science degree in Chemistry and Management from the University of the West Indies.

She is a mother of seven year old twin girls.

Audrey has been raising her twin daughters all alone since they were two months old, and is therefore the perfect person to share her coping strategies, from her personal experience.

TABLE OF CONTENTS

PREFACE 9

CHAPTER 1 – THE INITIAL SHOCK 13

CHAPTER 2 – THE FIRST SIX MONTHS 23

CHAPTER 3 – POTTY TRAINING 34

CHAPTER 4 – CONTROLLING MY RESENTMENT ... 40

CHAPTER 5 – CHILDHOOD ILLNESSES 46

CHAPTER 6 – A CLOSE EYE ON THE TWINS 53

CHAPTER 7 – TIME MANAGEMENT 60

CHAPTER 8 – MONEY MANAGEMENT 71

CHAPTER 9 – CREATIVE THINKING 79

CHAPTER 10 – TRAVELING OVERSEAS 85

CHAPTER 11 – ASKED FOR HELP 91

CHAPTER 12 – BOUNDARIES 97

CHAPTER 13 – TAKING CARE OF MYSELF 104

CHAPTER 14 – FOUGHT FOR MY TWINS 110

CHAPTER 15 – EXTRACURRICULAR ACTIVITIES.117

CHAPTER 16 – TACKLED BURNOUT 121

CHAPTER 16 – DEALING WITH TWIN COMPETITIVENESS..128

CHAPTER 17 – FINAL ANALYSIS.................................135

PREFACE

"How do you do it?"

This is a very common question that I'm asked quite often - by friends, family, fellow employees, and sometimes even strangers – on how I've managed to raise my twins all by myself, in a foreign country, with a full time job, limited money, and make it appear as if everything is under control. How is it that I have not fallen apart? In almost all the situations, once this question is asked by the interested party, there is great anticipation as the parent awaits my response.

In this book, I will share my very practical coping strategies, so that other single parents with twins; couples with twins; single parents with singlets; or any single parent or couple with multiple children of different ages, will be inspired and encouraged to raise their children successfully while coping with all the challenges around them.

Twins to One deals with the ratio of two children (and specifically twins) to one parent. It is important to examine the ratio of children to parent, because this translates into how much attention each child can get, expenses to care for them, and also to prevent 'burn out' of the parent. Many single parents, both mothers and fathers have singlehandedly taken care of multiple children all over the world, all the time. However, twins are another kettle of fish. Having two babies or two toddlers of the same age, with the same needs can be overwhelming to a couple, even when they have additional help. You can well imagine how difficult it is when there is only one parent with no help, especially when it is a new set of twins.

When I realized that I would be on my own, I started to scour the Internet to find practical and in-depth information on raising twin babies as a single parent. There was a lot of information on twin pregnancies - similarities between twins, what to expect when you're having twins and so forth - but nothing that was about my situation.

I decided to compile some of the most challenging and also some seemingly small, but significant things that I have experienced.

It should be noted that at the time this book was written, my twins were seven years old. I decided to write at this time, before I had forgotten some of the details of their earlier years. Therefore, all of my experiences are up to age seven years. This nevertheless, captures the most challenging times. I think that the most difficult years of raising my twins were the earliest.

I am not a psychologist, nor an expert on child rearing. That information may be gleaned from different websites and expert literature. I am, however, an experienced Registered Nurse in the Neonatal Intensive Care Unit (NICU), and as a single parent of twins, I have acquired the strategies set out in this book, to cope with all the demands of balancing work, school, and housework. You may choose areas that best suit you and your family.

CHAPTER 1 – THE INITIAL SHOCK

Do you recall the initial shock that you and your spouse or partner had, when you first heard that you were having twins? There aren't enough words in the English Language to express those emotions. My Obstetrician was so excited for me and my husband, and could barely contain his excitement when he exclaimed,

"There is the sac, and there is the baby. Oh wait. We have another sac and baby!"

I just lay on the examination bed of the ultrasound room as I was paralyzed with disbelief and happiness. I had always dreamed of having twins and a loving and supportive husband. And now, here I was, realizing my dream.

We were having identical twin girls!

Okay, I know that you may be curious as to how I came to be left alone, to raise my twin girls in a foreign country. So let me tell you in a nutshell.

As is usual, everything is lovely at the beginning of a relationship. After we got married, I moved to Bermuda, my husband's country.

Three years later, after planning to have a child, we got pregnant. My husband and I were so over the moon. He was there for the whole pregnancy. Even when I had the 'mask of pregnancy' where my face looked so unattractive, he seemed to have never noticed.

As I'd expected, and secretly wished, the babies were born at 34^{+5} weeks. As you know, 40 weeks is considered full term, so they were born about one month early, and I was relieved because they were so heavy that I had had to purchase a pregnancy sling for support for most of my pregnancy.

As a NICU Registered Nurse that had seen hundreds of deliveries, I had already decided to have a C-section. The method of birth is a very personal one, and no one should get to decided how a couple brings their baby into the world.

It was a good choice on my part to have a C-section though, because while Twin I was head down, and came out relatively quickly, Twin II was holding on for dear life to my liver! OK, not my liver. She was lying horizontally and high up in my abdomen.

Twin I was five pounds and four ounces, and Twin II was four pounds and eleven ounces.

The babies did well in the NICU, only spending two weeks there. The Pediatricians were happy to discharge premature babies who were feeding strongly, without the need for a feeding tube (NGT);

could maintain their body temperature without the need for an incubator; and had no infections and were gaining body weight.

When we took home our twin daughters, it was one of the happiest days of my life. I had two beautiful babies and a loving and supportive husband…….but only for a short time.

A few weeks after we got home, my husband became withdrawn. He did not want to help me with the babies. I was confused, but could not get the real reason from him for his behavior. It was not until after we had separated, and then divorced, that I got the full story – it had nothing to do with us. He had some very bad personal issues that he had kept secret, and the demand of the new babies had made it worse.

With the babies, only two months old, I left the marital home, as my ex-husband's behavior was not conducive to a good environment. I didn't know where I was going, and he thought that I would be back. After all, I had no family in Bermuda, my parents were deceased, and I had very little money, a C-section wound that was not fully healed, a raging custody battle, and two young babies.

The initial shock of what had just happened, of feeling abandoned, with no idea of where I was going to live, was just as overwhelming as when I had learnt that I was having twins. Only this time, it was unpleasantly overwhelming. How was I going to manage on my own? The shock soon turned into feeling scared and vulnerable. Then intense anger.

I quickly realized that I could not stay in this angry place. It would serve no good to my twin babies, and certainly not to me.

This was the point where I decided that I had to prepare myself for some very challenging times ahead.

Self-Talk

This was the most important part of my coping strategies. I had to reprogram my mind if I were going to survive on my own, and create a 'normal' life for my twins. I decided that I was going to be more tired than the average parent. I decided that I had to have a certain mindset.

I spoke to myself every day. I was temporarily staying at a 'safe house', as I was on no paid maternity leave, and did not have enough money to rent a proper apartment. Because the babies were unaware of what I was actually doing, I literally spoke out loudly to myself. I voiced that I would not allow myself to get so depressed, as I would not be able to take care of myself, or my twins. I prayed to God to keep me from going under – every day.

Got an Attorney (Legal Aid)

I got a Legal Aid attorney for the two months of no paid maternity leave period only. I made note of most of the details of what had happened in my marriage that led up to me leaving. This would come in handy when writing the affidavit to present my case to the courts for supervised visits, or custody matters, and divorce.

I even wrote some of my affidavits in the beginning of the divorce and custody matters. All my then attorney had to do, was to read what I had written. On one occasion, I had asked my attorney to ask the judge for supervised visits. His response was that there was no way a judge would be willing to grant such a request without compelling reasons. Now, because I had made great notes shortly after the incidents when they were fresh in my mind, it was easy to recall all the reasons for supervised visits to the twins' father.

My attorney could not believe his ears in the court room, when the judge granted supervised visits based on my 'compelling reasons' or evidence. My win started to build up my confidence.

Found Some Normalcy

I knew I had to quickly get over the initial shock of what had just happened in the relationship. For the sake of the children and myself, I knew I had to find stability somehow.

Just before I returned to work, I asked as many people as possible to help me find a babysitter that I could afford. I also started looking for a 'reasonably priced' apartment. I borrowed a substantial amount of money from a close friend to buy some used and new furniture. And for the time being, I could only afford one crib for both babies.

Informed My Workplace

Finally, I told my manager, without going into too much details, about my situation. This was because of a change in my immigration status, and also for traveling arrangements for frequent business meetings. Your workplace needs to know that your status has changed. By status, I mean that you are not married anymore, and therefore have limited support as a single parent now. Your immigration status could also affect your work and residency status. I was at a point in my life where everything was tenuous.

In Bermuda, if you are a non-Bermudian spouse of a Bermudian, and your marriage breaks down before you have attained the time of 10 years, you could be asked to leave the country, unless there are other circumstances.

In my situation, I was not asked to leave the island, but I had to get a temporary Work Permit, until the application of my new status was finalized. After I had informed my manager, she directed Human Resources to sort out my immigration status.

I had let HR know that I would need to travel with my babies to the business meetings, as I had no one to leave them with in Bermuda. Besides the twins were being breastfed. My company allowed me to bring my twins, and I made sure that once I was in the business sessions for that week, that I gave them my full focus.

Even if your immigration status is not relevant in your country, it would still be a good idea to inform your company, in order to deal with some personal matters that may come up, such as visiting the courts.

And just remember, most companies will accommodate you, but you are still expected to function on some level. I believe that my company knew that once my twins were safe and ok, that I would be calmer and more focused.

CHAPTER 2 – THE FIRST SIX MONTHS

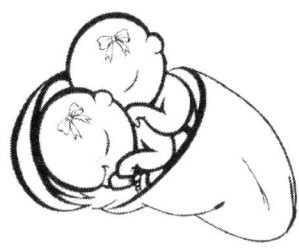

For the first two months, while I was still with my husband, I would breastfeed one of the twins, while he would bottle feed the other with my expressed breastmilk. I would alternate the twins for their next feeding time. But after the demise of the marriage, I was on my own with two relatively small babies to breastfeed at the same time.

All that teaching that I had done with hundreds of mothers with twins, on 'the football hold' for feeding their twin babies simultaneously, did not work for me. Go figure.

Bottle and Breastfed the Twins Simultaneously

So I had to come up with a plan. I put one twin in a neck pillow, just like the ones you use for traveling on an airplane. Then I would feed her from a bottle with my right hand. I would then cradle the second twin in my left arm, bringing her to my breast. It was a bit awkward at first, not to mention uncomfortable, but that was the best I could do.

The more I practiced feeding both twins at the same time, the more comfortable I got. I started fantasizing about the day when my babies would be able to take their bottles from me, and feed themselves.

It wasn't long before my dreams were realized, because children grow up.

Milk Supplements

And speaking of breastfeeding, because of my high level of stress and sadness, my breast milk production understandably slowed down. I had no appetite, and that did not bode well for the amount of calories needed to be consumed for a breastfeeding mother. According to the American College of Obstetricians and Gynecologists, breastfeeding mothers need approximately 2,500 calories per day.[1]

I did not stress too much about the fact that I was not producing enough milk. Although I knew that breastmilk was superior to formula, the latter has used for decades, and is also full of nutrients for even premature babies. The common ones we used at the hospitals were Similac and Enfamil. I bought the formula at a wholesale store for more efficient use of my limited funds. I started alternating the babies with breastmilk and formula. They were

---

[1] https://www.acog.org/Patients/FAQs/Breastfeeding-Your-Baby

gaining weight consistently and were quite healthy, according to their Pediatrician.

Baby Monitor

After I moved into a modestly priced apartment, found by a friend of a friend, and started to have a more constructive life and routine, I knew that I had to closely monitor the twins as they had *infant reflux*, or gastroesophageal reflux (GER). They were spitting up a lot. I had returned to work. One of my sisters bought me a baby monitor with camera and sound. This piece of equipment gave me some piece of mind. I would watch them every night until I finally fell asleep. It was this baby monitor that alerted me one late evening of one of my twins' seizures. I will explain a little later.

Infantile Colic 'Cure'

In the first few months, some babies, and more so premature babies, present with infantile colic. This is when a baby starts to cry, usually in the late afternoon, and does so for several hours.[2] This crying is inconsolable. They would both be pulling up their legs towards their tummies. And worse, they would both be crying at the same time. And for most of those days, the crying would go on until 2:00 am!

It was one of my worst experiences being on my own. It started in the 'safe house' when the twins were two months old. Both babies would suddenly start to cry at around 5:00 pm. Nothing seemed to work. I warmed their milk a little more to see whether that would calm their tummies, and that did not help. I gave them *Ovol* drops or gripe water, and still nothing. Walked around with them. Nothing.

Even though I was beyond exhausted, I told myself that my twin babies must be having the most

---

[2]https://en.wikipedia.org/wiki/Baby_colic

excruciating tummy pains, not unlike my period pains. With this empathy for my babies, I did not lose it. Finally, I tried to do some 'bicycle moving' exercises with their legs. I would alternate the babies. The crying became less intense, and seemed to be working. I practiced this for the two months that the colic lasted. I have no idea how it worked, or if that were even what reduced their colicky pains, but I was glad that their suffering had diminished.

Stimulation

According to neuroscientist Audrey van der Meer, a professor at the Norwegian University of Science and Technology (NTNU), "modern brain research shows that early stimulation contributes to brain development gains even in the wee ones among us."[3] This new research is in stark contrast to the old

---

[3]https://www.sciencedaily.com/releases/2017/01/170102143458.htm

adage that babies should be left alone to naturally develop.

So I set out to employ different methods for stimulation of my twin daughters. I employed a number of strategies. Although I did not have a lot of money, I bought a very colorful crib mobile with night lights and soothing music. They seemed to enjoy it. I was not in the mood to talk much, but I tried. The words came scarcely at first, and with tears, but as I persisted, they flowed more. I spoke to them like I would an older child – I did no baby talking. I read to them daily, and they seemed to like that. They loved hearing my voice.

At ages six and seven years, my twin daughters have been receiving awards for several of their subject areas, especially for English Language.

One thing that never left me, and I did not have to struggle to do, was singing. And since I can sing pretty well, I often sang to them, as well as for myself. Now at age seven years, both my twins sing pretty well, if I may say so myself.

Photos and Videos

With all the stress of court, and so many demands on my time as a new single mother with twins, the last thing I was thinking of, was to savor the moments. It was one of my sisters that had reminded me, and then she had sent me a camera, which was also able to do videotaping. I will always be grateful for her nudge, because I have captured some very precious moments of me and my twins.

So one thing you should never forget to do, is to take photos and videos of your babies at every stage. No matter what is going on in your life – take photos. Most phones are able to take at least a decent enough photo or video.

Now that my twin daughters are seven years old, I have all their photos and videos from the C-section delivery to them being in the NICU, to being at home, their first walk, and their first words. I have pictures of every one of their birthdays. I feel so much gratitude to see where my twins and I have come from, to now.

After all the drama has stopped, and the custody battle is over, you will be glad that you have wonderful memories of your twins' monthly and yearly developments. Remember that twins are not that common. They and you are special. Looking back, if I had not done videos of my twins crawling, taking their first steps, running, playing 'hide and seek' with each other, I would have been extremely disappointed in myself. So remember to take pictures.

Tennis Elbows

Single parents with twins, or even with multiple children at different ages, have a very hard time managing everything else in our lives, while taking care of our children. We have to shop with the children; take them to the Pediatrician all by ourselves; visit the lawyers' offices and other business places with them; and the list goes on. I have seen strong fathers at the Pediatrician's office just easily lift up twin babies' car seats to bring them into the office.

Well, I was on my own, so I had to lift two babies and take them to see the Pediatrician as well. I would never leave my babies in the car, not even to grab something quickly. I was carrying both babies in their car seats, one in each hand several times a day. After a few months, one day a sudden excruciating pain shot through both elbows. I almost dropped my babies!

My GP said that I had developed tennis elbow (lateral epicondylitis). I was referred to an orthopedic surgeon who wanted to give me steroid injections in the joints. I refused and accepted ultrasound treatment which was less invasive, and quite effective. The ultrasound sent pulses to the damaged tendon. The surgeon also prescribed anti-inflammatory medications. The medications and ultrasound worked well to relieve most of the pain over the next few months. I tried afterwards, whenever possible, to take the twins out of their car seats, as the seats increased the weight that I had to carry.

CHAPTER 3 – POTTY TRAINING

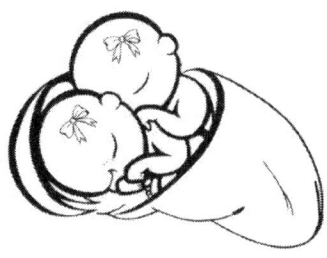

I am unsure as to why I was so anxious about potty training from the time the twins were just a few months old. I had known of a few older children, even up to age twelve years, who were still wetting their beds. Plus, after I was on my own with the twins, I wondered how I would be able to potty train two babies simultaneously. I feared that it would be worse than breastfeeding both babies simultaneously. I also felt like it was going to be a challenge because the apartment I had rented, was fully carpeted. The smell of urine and the mess of stool on carpet is certainly a headache.

Beautiful Potties

On one of my business trips to Florida, I had gone to Walmart and had bought two beautiful potties. They were pink and seemed sturdy. They had covers that when closed, doubled as a stool for the twins to reach up to the bathroom sink! They were quite inexpensive, even for me at that time.

The twins loved their potties, and were willing to sit on them for practice. I started putting them on the potties several times a day, even though they were still in diapers.

By the time the twins were almost two years old, they had started to sit on their potties without resistance.

But not once did I force them. I simply encouraged them.

I then decided to graduate my toddlers to the regular toilet. I had seen and read how some parents had put their toddlers on the toilet to acclimatize them to it. Fearing that my twins would fall into the toilet, I had bought a child seat and put it over the regular toilet seat. I put the twins on the toilet during the daytime, and allowed them to use their potties at night, which I had placed beside their toddler beds.

By the time my twins were three years old, they were using the toilet without the child seat.

Bedwetting

After my twins were fully potty trained, they began to have bedwetting incidents. I acted as though it was no big deal, as I did not want them to feel self-conscious. I had started to wake them up in the middle of the night, but it was proving to be too tiring. I started putting them in night-time diapers. I was surprised at how the twins were embarrassed that they still needed 'diapers'. I explained to them that even some adults have to wear diapers at times, and that they would soon not be needing them.

But I was beginning to feel anxious again, when some wise person asked me,

"Have you ever seen a teenager wetting her bed?"

Ok, good point.

Since the twins are older now, I have limited their fluids to no later than 5:30 pm since their bedtime is at 8:00 pm. That has worked wonders, and the accidents are rare now.

Smelly Mattresses

The scent of a six or seven year old child's urine is very different from the cute little urine scent of a baby's. It's really bad when an older child has a bedwetting accident. I was really frustrated with being unable to remove the scent once, and did not like the fumes from the bleach. So I had gone online to the GhostBed site where I found the following method of removal, very helpful:

1. To get out the stench of the urine smell you will want to use the vinegar full strength. Spraying the vinegar soak the areas of the mattress that have been affected by the urine. For tough stained area use a toothbrush to rub the vinegar in. Open the windows and run a fan as you let the vinegar set for five to 10-minutes.
2. Using layers of fresh paper toweling soak up the vinegar from the mattress.
3. Take the baking soda and sprinkle it over stained areas until covered. Now take a break to let the baking soda set in for at least a couple of hours. Leave the soda on spots for as long as possible. The baking soda will begin to clump up as it soaks in the vinegar. This is what removes the vinegar along with odor.
4. Use your vacuum to clean up the dried baking soda from the mattress going over the bed until all the soda is removed[4]

---

[4] https://www.ghostbed.com/education/how-to-remove-urine-from-your-mattress/

Surprisingly, potty training my twin daughters was not as scary, or as tiring as I had thought it would be. I was also very glad to have stopped buying so many diapers (for two toddlers).

CHAPTER 4 – CONTROLLING MY RESENTMENT

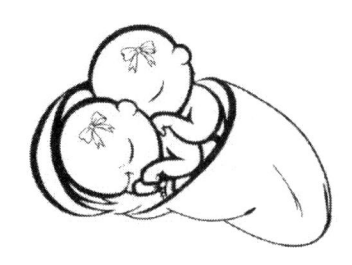

When my ex-husband realized that I had no intention of returning to the marriage, he launched a harassment campaign, through the courts. Every time I was to travel for a business meeting overseas, he would refuse to sign the permission papers for me to travel with the babies, even when they were newborns that were being breastfed. He also tried to get sole custody of the twins, even though he had no compelling reasons, excepting that 'I was very obsessed with the twins'. This back and forth in court caused me to incur huge legal fees, while he was paying almost nothing towards the care of the babies. Additionally, I had learnt that he was going around and telling stories about me that he had concocted.

All of these negative behaviors and more, enraged me, and I eventually grew, to not just resent my ex-husband, but to actually hate him.

I know that many of the single parents, fathers and mothers, have similar stories. However, I am not disclosing my story for any other reason, than to say that you have to control your resentment for the sake of your twins. Many parents often use their children as pawns, and in a contest for their own egos. But the short-term victories will, in the long run, damage their children.

No Bad-mouthing of Ex with My Twins

Although I was filled with resentment, I made a conscious effort not to say anything negative about my ex-husband around or to my twins about their father. It was super hard to control myself.

But most parents would do anything for their children. Barring things that are illegal or immoral, I would do anything for my twin daughters. So if not speaking negatively of my ex would protect my twins, then I was going to do everything I could to refrain from doing that.

As you already know, children often pretend as though they are not hearing or understanding your conversations, when they actually are. I know, because after my conversations on the phone, my twins would sometimes ask me what I had meant by certain phrases. It always shocked me, because at those times, they seemed so engrossed in what they were doing, way over the other side of the room!

After my ex-husband had left the island for good, he would call the twins. He had not said when he would return and neither did he help financially. It was very hard over those years paying all the bills, loans, and trying to play the part of two parents. Whenever he called the twins, he would tell them how much he loved them, and how he would return to the island soon. It took great restraint not to roll my eyes during his 'performances' but I looked at my twin daughters' faces, and they believed every word that their father was telling them. I knew it was good for their self-esteem, that their dad was taking the time to call them. So I supported my twins at the end of each phone call to say,

"See. Your daddy loves you very much."

No Fighting In Front of My Twins

I also told my ex-husband, when he was initially collecting the twins for his court assigned time with them, that I would tolerate no fighting in front of the twins. This was after he had attempted to question a comment I had made to one of his friends. He began to get upset, raising his voice. I stopped him right there, and told him in no uncertain terms, to never, ever, start a fight with me again, in front of the twins.

According to the findings of a research that was published in the *Journal of Psychopathology*, "children who hear or witness their parents fighting may have trouble regulating their emotions in less risky situations, such as a classroom."[5]

I Never Criticize My Twins

It is easy to resort to displacing your resentment of your exes, onto the children. You could end up criticizing your children, which is a passive aggressive behavior for getting back at your exes. I

---
[5] https://steinhardt.nyu.edu/site/ataglance/2014/09/fighting-parents-hurt-childrens-ability-to-regulate-emotions-finds-study-by-psychologists-at-nyu-steinhardt.html

promised myself to never criticize my twins. I believe it is easy to criticize your children, especially if the twins look almost completely like the other parent, as in my case.

At every step of the way, I took my twin daughters into consideration. I wanted my twins to be as unaffected by having a single parent as they could possibly be. They had nothing to do with the demise of the marriage.

I have always tried to remember to tell my twins that I did not like their behavior. I try to say,

"That behavior is naughty," instead of,

"You are naughty."

CHAPTER 5 – CHILDHOOD ILLNESSES

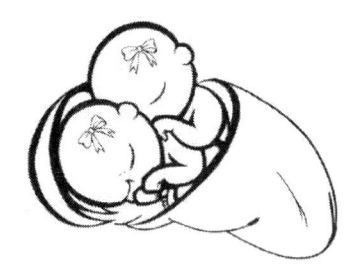

Children build up their immune system when they are exposed to the different illnesses caused by viruses, bacteria, and fungus. All parents are aware of this information. However, when the child is ill and uncomfortable because he has a cold, or the flu, and cannot breathe properly, the illness period can take a toll on the parents. They cannot sleep or eat properly, and the same for you. You know that your child feels horrible, he does not want to eat anything, and resists taking his medicine for his fever. This drives many parents crazy because you cannot take away the child's discomfort. In the case of a viral infection, such as the flu, you can only treat the symptoms like the fever and headache that it causes. However, you will have to wait until the virus 'self-limits'. That is, the virus limits its own growth after it has run its course.

As an R.N., I was not fazed by the common cold or flu whenever my twins got ill. However, I was rattled by some complications of the flu.

Febrile Seizures

The twins were two and a half years old and both had got the flu. I had given them children's Advil for their moderately high fever, and put them to bed. A little later in the night, I heard a weird sound from the twins' room, and I looked at the baby monitor. I noticed some strange movements from Twin I in her crib (I had bought an additional crib when they were one year old), and rushed into their room. There I saw Twin I having convulsions. She was blue, and frothing at the mouth. In that moment I was shaken up, as I had only learnt about febrile seizures, but had never actually witnessed it.

I picked her up and she was extremely hot. I took off all her clothes and sponged her down. Her temperature was 104 °F (40 °C). I called 911 for the ambulance, and continued to sponge her down. My heart was racing. I checked Twin II. She was still asleep. I had no one to call. It was approximately 7:00 pm. I had to wake Twin II up to ride with me in the ambulance. The EMTs got an IV in Twin I's arm to give her some fluids to cool her core temperature down. Her temperature had shot up to 107 °F (42 °C) on their thermometer!

When the ambulance arrived at the Emergency Room, I was relieved. The IV fluids were quickly reducing my daughter's high temperature. They also gave her some more *Advil* and alternated it with *Tylenol*. Twin I went on to have two more febrile seizures a year later.

While I was sitting by Twin I's bed in the ER, and at the same time watching Twin II, I did not notice that the doctor was paying attention to me. I was feeling really unwell and I had a cough. The doctor asked me whether I was having chills and insisted that I go do an x-ray. I refused, but the nurses chimed in. I obliged while the staff promised to supervise the twins in ER until I had returned.

The x-rays showed the beginning of a pneumonia, and I was prescribed antibiotics immediately.

The next two days, as Twin I was recovering from the flu, Twin II had a similar episode of febrile seizures. I did the same thing again and was back in the ER again, with both twins. On both occasions, I was leaving for my home from the ER at 2:00 am or 3:00 am. I kept telling myself that that situation was only for a time. Most children 'outgrow' febrile seizures around the age of five or six years old. Self-talk was really helpful at those difficult times.

Gastroenteritis

All parents know that their young children will have vomiting and diarrhea from time to time, from gastroenteritis or from other causes. Whenever this happened, it did not faze me as an RN. If my twins kept on vomiting, then I would use Pediatric *Gravol* suppositories that are sold over-the-counter. They are very effective in reducing nausea, and could control the actual vomiting. If that was not very effective, as in a few cases, then I would go to the ER for rehydration with IV fluids.

Strep Throat and Rheumatic Fever

And because I was alone with the twins, I would never take chances. One such childhood illness that I am always vigilant about is Strep throat. This is a highly contagious throat infection that is caused by the Streptococcal bacteria. It can be easily spread through airborne droplets from someone's cough or sneeze.[6]

The reason for my vigilance is because of the rare possibility that there could be the complication of *rheumatic fever*. This can cause painful joints, and swelling, but of greatest concern to me, is the damage that it can do to the heart valves. So, once my twins complain of a sore throat, I immediately check for white dots or patches in the back of your throat. I also check their tonsils, the fleshy structures on either side at the back of their throat, to see if they are red and swollen. The WebMD site has a slide show of what Strep. Throat may look like.[7]

---

[6] https://www.mayoclinic.org/diseases-conditions/strep-throat/symptoms.../syc-20350338
[7] https://www.webmd.com/cold-and-flu/ss/slideshow-anatomy-of-a-sore-throat

If I am unsure, I take the twins straight to their Pediatrician or to The Clinic, if I do not have enough money.

CHAPTER 6 – A CLOSE EYE ON THE TWINS

It is a no brainer that your home should be prepared for your crawling twin babies, but more so for your toddlers who are now walking. This is obviously for all parents to do. But for a single parent with twins, this imperative.

Made Some Space in My Home

Once the twins had started to walk, my apartment had a look of starkness - a couch, a recliner, TV, and a rug in the center with an ottoman as the coffee table. This was to provide as much space as possible for toddlers that never stopped running and falling. I kept my sliding doors closed and only opened the top sections of the windows.

Toddler-proofed My Home

I removed all breakables within the twins' reach. I used tie-downs on the TV stand that had doors, and all the kitchen cupboards that had 'dangerous' chemicals in them. I covered all the electrical outlets with transparent plugs. And I was so glad that I had done that, when I caught one of the twins fiddling with it.

Now I know some people may be rolling their eyes here, but when you are a single parent, you cannot afford to take chances. Just as you are paying attention to one twin, the other is doing something she should not be doing.

And as for keeping a close eye, I was shocked one day when the twins were about eighteen months old, and I had temporarily strapped them into their twin stroller. I was wiping the floor and did not want them to fall. I was shocked when I felt two tiny hands hugging my legs!

"How did you get out of your stroller?" I asked her as she giggled with glee.

She had figured out how to squeeze the buckles and pull out the strap. By two years old, the twins were scaling the top of their cribs like prisoners escaping a prison wall. I had to put soft and fluffy bed stuff at the foot of their cribs on the floor.

Leashes for the Twins

With the twins walking, I would ensure, when traveling through the airports, that I attached leashes on them. I particularly liked the teddy bear ones that looked like a backpack. I would then put the other ends of their leaches through my belt. It is hard enough for two parents to travel overseas with their children, but almost a nightmare for a single parent with twins. They could run off in different directions.

Wary of Strangers

My twin daughters often wanted to play outside, especially when they were about four years old. But I also kept my eyes on them from inside the apartment. One of those days when the girls were playing outside, I noticed a man passing by the wall of my apartment with a very tiny dog on a leash. The wall of the apartment was very high, and reached up to the level of a tall adult's shoulders. When the passerby noticed my twins out in the yard, he suddenly stopped and placed his tiny dog on top of the wall, while saying.

"Girls. Hi girls."

My twin daughters, even though I had told them not to talk to strangers, were so excited to see the dog, started towards the wall. I immediately came out on to the patio and called out for them to come inside. The man seemed very surprised that I was there and immediately grabbed his tiny dog off the wall and disappeared. I do not know if this man was a pedophile or what, but I have very little trust for most people, especially when my twins were younger.

Eyes Wide Open at the Beach

Every parent already knows that they are to watch their children at the beach. But for a single parent of identical twins, I was even more vigilant. Sometimes I would look up, and my eyes would play tricks on me. Was it Twin I that I just saw over there, or was it Twin II? My twins, like many children, love the water, and I allow them to enjoy it. But unless I am accompanied by a friend that can swim, I do not swim. I either sit on the beach, or stand in the water while watching them. It takes a minute for an accident to happen, and since I am alone with the twins at the beach most of the time, I would rather be bored than sorry. I sacrificed and had them go for almost an entire summer of swimming lessons when they were six years old, and thereafter. This was just to give me more peace of mind for summer camps or school trips, when I could not be there.

Device Monitoring

The twins now seven years old, are really into their devices, so I keep my eyes on what they watch. It is hard, as I cannot watch them constantly. So I explain to them that sometimes the characters on some of the games, could actually be teenagers or adults pretending to be children. These persons may say inappropriate things to them through texts. I instruct them not to text or comment on anything.

I also explain to my girls; that they can be bullied on the Internet. I had shown them an animated video of two children being bullied on a game on their computer by other children. I set up their tablets with mine by using only my account. Doing this allows me to see which videos they were on.

Now the twins let me know every time someone tries to contact them on these games, or tries to bully them.

CHAPTER 7 – TIME MANAGEMENT

The most common questions I get from couples and other single parents, is about how I manage my time.

All parents struggle with the pull of the different aspects of our lives. All of them are demanding of our time – our children, job, housework, school, friends, family, housework, recreation, and taking care of ourselves (like grooming).

The difficulty comes about because it is hard to prioritize, when all of these different demands have to be met on some level. As usual, this is hard for couples with children, so one can just imagine how hard it is for a single parent of twins.

To Do List

Firstly, I try to budget my day – every single day. I have a to-do-list on my phone for each day of the week. Because I have so many different things that must be done, and I am always forgetting, since I am so tired, I write them down as soon as I remember. This is an actual example:

To-do-list

November 22, 2017

1. Buy gas
2. Make client appointments
3. Put money under Twin I's pillow for the Tooth Fairy
4. Call telephone company re: Internet
5. Supermarket
6. Return call to sister.

I write every single thing that is outstanding. I don't care if they are in order. I just want to get them done on that particular day. As soon as I have completed a task, I delete it from my list.

My to-do-lists make me appear efficient, and keeps me together. I did not make a note on my list recently of replacing one of my twins' tooth with money. I forgot twice. My daughter was so disappointed. I told her that she is to just wrap the tooth in a piece of tissue, instead of putting it in a

Ziploc bag. I then promptly entered the reminder in my to-do-list. The next morning, I remembered only because I had checked my list. My twin was so excited,

"Mommy the Tooth Fairy finally came and took my tooth. She left me $2!"

My clients are sometimes surprised that I honor my promises to bring something to them, such as information that they had asked for. As soon as I leave my clients' offices, I make a note of whatever they need from me, right outside their offices.

Budgeted My Time

In addition to my daily to-do-list, I also estimate how much time I would need to dress my twins and myself, eat our meals, and drive to the venue or appointment. It may seem anal, but being a single parent with twins, does not give you any passes. The Pediatrician's office is not going to excuse your thirty minutes of lateness because you had no help getting your twins ready. Your friends are not going to wait for you and your children to arrive at their kid's birthday party two hours late, because they understand that you may have had some difficulties at home with your twins. The world will not stop for me, and it hasn't. So I have employed this method, from the time I was left to raise my twins, all by myself at two months old, to present.

My respect for time, even as a single parent of twins, has not only inspired other parents, but has also made me a role model to my twin daughters on how to be respectful of other people's time.

Lunch Planning

Deciding what you are going to send as meal for your children every day to school, can make most parents pull out their hair. It irks us when the children return from school with their lunches untouched. Good planning can help relieve this.

I decide from the beginning of each week, what I will give my twins for lunch each day of the week. I have even incorporated their input to see what they would enjoy.

This lunch plan, greatly reduced my stress when I was getting my toddlers ready for daycare, and now school, that they are older.

Clothes Planning

I do the same for their clothes as I do for their lunches. Although this seems insignificant, not knowing what my twins were going to wear in a time crunch, could suddenly increase my stress levels, and could even make me late for my appointment. And yes, I still dress them alike, when they allow me to. Sometimes I have tried to buy different styles, but they both want the same one of the two styles, so I have reverted to the same style for their clothes. During the summer holidays, I let them choose what they want to wear. And no surprise, sometimes they choose the same outfits.

Homework

The last thing I want is for my twins' performances to fall through the cracks, and for society to say that that it is because they are from a single-family home. I do not want my children to be patronized, only to be respected.

Although I am a single parent, my twin daughters excel at every level in their school work. I make it very clear to my twins that I expect them to try their very best. I do not allow them to play outside, watch TV, or play on their devices, until they have completed their homework.

Homework or reviewing their classwork for tests, is a priority. They get the option of having a snack first or doing their homework first. So I put my bags down and proceed to help my twins. It becomes very challenging here as they both want me to assist them at the same time. I explain to them that I will alternate between them, and that I am only one person. For all the subjects, I explain the different topics to them at their level, and then I create practice tests, or copy the ones the teachers send home. This method has worked very well for my twins.

Time with My Twins

Although my time is extremely limited, I make sure to spend some time with my twin daughters. It is not easy, but I get creative with it. I'll discuss this in more details later in my book. If you are a single parent, and you are too busy to spend time with your children, you could permanently affect them. "The importance of this time is multifold:

1. The child feels important and loved.
2. He or she has an opportunity to model parent's behavior.

3. The parent can observe and learn about the child's strengths and weaknesses in order to better guide them.
4. The child has a chance to voice their thoughts and feelings.
5. The parent and child develop a stronger bond."[8]

For years, as a young child, I tried to get the attention of my father. I felt like he was a very good provider, but I did not get enough one on one with him. He was a builder and carpenter. In order to bond with my father, I had asked him to teach me carpentry. Although he obliged me, I think that I had to work really hard for his attention. I try very hard to not let history repeat itself.

---

[8]https://childdevelopmentinfo.com/psychology/importance-of-family-time-on-kids-mental-health-and-adjustment-to-life/

Compartmentalized My Focus

Compartmentalizing my time is also another way in which I manage my time as a single parent. I give 100% to my job, after I drop off my twins at school. I even received the Representative of the Year for outstanding performance, along with other excellence awards. I focus on my clients completely at work.

Once at home, I turn off the work mode. I concentrate on my twins, housework, homework, and meals. Once I have done all of that, and I have put my twins to bed, I take some 'me time' before I go to sleep. My 'me time' is the time when I can properly talk to my family, friends, watch my favorite TV show, or write a book.

I Learned To Say 'No'

Now, as all parents know, people are always making demands of our time, especially schools, community, and church. I learned to say a resounding 'no' to anything that I knew I was unable to give 100% to, or anything that just cannot fit into my time budget – without feeling any guilt. If you have a problem saying no, then you'll have to practice it. Rationalize it. If you are going to feel resentful for agreeing to do something, then it is unhealthy. I have practiced saying 'no' and now I do not feel guilty. I am just one person, but more so, just one parent with twins.

CHAPTER 8 – MONEY MANAGEMENT

Every family has to manage its finances, whether there is sufficient amount of money or not. However, it becomes more difficult for single parents, and especially those with multiple children like me.

I have had a modestly paying job which was enough while I was married. However, with the demise of my marriage, and my now ex-husband causing me to incur huge legal fees, as well as starting over, my salary suddenly was stretched too thinly. It was then that I had to employ some strategies.

Bermuda has the highest cost of living in the world according to the data company Numbeo which published its Cost of Living Index Rate for 2017.[9] And has also been one of the most expensive countries in the whole world, according to The Organization for Economic Co-operation and Development (OECD) for previous years.

Negotiated Payments

You can well imagine how difficult it was to balance my budget. When the twins were two years old, my ex-husband, after dragging me through court, and getting joint custody, suddenly up and left Bermuda. The twins were then toddlers and were in daycare. Daycare cost per child was about US$1000. I had asked several persons to help me find a new daycare,

---

[9] https://www.numbeo.com/cost-of-living/rankings_current.jsp

as I thought their cost would be a bit lower. When I had found such a daycare, I met with the owner and requested a 'sibling rate', explaining my situation. She agreed.

Fortunately, my job offered good, but expensive health insurance. When the twins were younger, they were frequently ill, or just going for their milestone assessments, immunizations, visits to the dentist, hearing assessments, ER visits. Most of these had a copayment. Sometimes, I would just ask the Pediatrician's office to put the copayment on my account. This would give me some time to pay.

Government Clinic

When I absolutely had insufficient money and the twins were ill, I would sometimes use the Department of Health or Government Clinic. It was just as good as the Pediatrician's office, but the waiting time was long, and the twins would become restless. But I would often pay nothing upfront.

Clothes as Gifts

As for clothes for the twins, I would request that my friends or family, give the girls clothes for their birthday and Christmas, whenever they offered a gift. I did not buy too much clothes for my twins as they were growing very fast between the ages of one to five years. During the early years of my twins, I bought almost no clothes, a sacrifice that I had to make, since the industry in which I work expects you to be well groomed.

And speaking of grooming, I did my own hair, nails, and was creative with my makeup.

Refinanced My Loans

Being single does not give you a pass to be irresponsible. You have to pay your bills. I have always paid all my bills, and on time. Even when my salary could not cover all my expenses, I would pay my rent, car loan, daycare fees, and utility bills first. And when I really could not afford my bank loan payments, I went in and spoke with one of the bank representatives. Because of my consistency of making my monthly loan repayments, the bank was willing to refinance my loan to a rate and amount that I could afford. I didn't even know that the bank would have actually done that for me, but I did not want to default on my loan. This responsible action on my part served me well in the eyes of the bank. It was also easier for me to get another loan a few years later, to pay off my legal fees, and secure a more reasonable rate than what was offered by the law firm.

Education Fund

Although I could barely find money for groceries, I was concerned about my twins' education. I enrolled in an education fund for tertiary education and started putting a very small amount towards their education. Believe me, the amounts were unimpressive, but I felt a little sense of relief that I had at least started. After the legal issues were sorted out, and I had settled all my fees, I increased the payment amounts of the education fund.

Even with the increase, I know the monthly donations are still not sufficient for both of my twins, but as I have stated, there is less anxiety now that I have started.

Strategic Grocery Shopping

Affording groceries was a challenge, especially during the height of the court cases. I tried to stretch the small amount allocated for it. I would buy groceries weekly, or even twice a week, in order to prevent waste. This strategy was really helpful. And when that was still not enough, I would ask my family overseas for help. My credit card also came in handy. I would pay more than the minimum payments, and after the due dates, would use the card again.

Overseas Trips

I would only take a trip for business meetings. And since I had no one to leave my children with, I would always take them with me, along with a sitter. My company would pay all my expenses for the trip, and I would pay for my twins and the sitter – airfare and hotel accommodation. It was rough and not to mention expensive. I would take salary advances from my company at times, to cover the trip. The one thing that would come out of it was that the twins would have a great time. Their last trip in The Bahamas, when the company used The Atlantis Hotel for the business meeting, they had a whale of a time on the water slides and other fun events. I felt so good that at the least, my twins get to have a few enjoyable trips. However, for me, I have not let my hair down since they were born. But I have resigned myself to not having a trip until and unless, I can truly afford it. It's the sacrifice I have to make for being a single parent, on my own, with twins.

Finally, I stretched out my hair appointments to save money, and I only did my nails at the salon when I had a special occasion or when going on business trips.

CHAPTER 9 – CREATIVE THINKING

All parents can agree that our time is limited for all the things we need to accomplish, and yet still find quality time to spend with our kids.

Cooking Assistants

I do not always have absolute time to set aside everything that I am doing, to just be with my twin daughters. So I often incorporate them into some of the other things that I am doing. For instance, whenever I am cooking, I would have them 'assist' me. One twin will be breaking the eggs into a bowl, while the other is turning the pancakes. You should see the pride on the faces of my five and six year old twins.

Now that they are seven years old, they can actually prepare some of their own meals, while I am in the kitchen washing the dishes. I just turn on the stove and let them be the chefs. They can cook, without any help, macaroni and cheese, pancakes, scrambled eggs, and rice. And of course, they can warm their milk for their cereal. I have noticed that they tend to eat their food in its entirety when they prepare it.

I've achieved two goals in a common time - my twins' self-confidence have been boosted, and we have spent some quality time together.

Gym Possible

A parent of two small kids once asked me how I found time to work out at the gym. I told her that I have no nanny or babysitter, so I take my twins to school or camp, and head straight to the gym, twice a week for an hour. When school is out, I sometimes take them with me, and have them watch their devices in the waiting room, supervised by the receptionist, while I work out. By working out, I keep myself healthy so that I can have some energy to take care of my twins, and at the same time, I am a good role model for them.

Creative Time Together

I have also had to be creative when I had projects to do, such as writing my first book. The book writing was very time consuming, so I had to get creative again. Sometimes the twins were just happy to be in my presence. I would make sure that we were all in the same room while writing, and them watching their devices quietly, or reading books. Again, achieving two things with the same common time.

Horseback Riding

At the age of five years, my twin daughters were exposed to one lesson of horseback riding by a friend. After that, my twins decided that they wanted to have horseback riding lessons.

But this is Bermuda.

It would cost US$60 per 30 minutes per child! Then I would have to buy boots, helmets, and the appropriate clothes. I knew that I would definitely not be able to afford it. But then it dawned on me that I could use an equestrian student. I found one and she charged me US$25 per hour per child! Still, I was glad when the lessons stopped due to something about the horse's feet. Although she was much cheaper, I was still finding it hard to afford the lessons. However, I was glad that the twins were exposed to horseback riding.

Rearranged my Housework

My twin daughters kept bugging me to enroll them in extracurricular activities. I was becoming more and more exhausted and kept deferring. But at age seven, they became insistent that they wanted to do activities on Saturdays. That was a dreaded request. I did everything on Saturdays. I washed all the clothes; folded all the clothes, ironed for the week; washed their hair and styled them; washed my hair; cooked, and shop for groceries or anything needed for the house. Every Saturday I was totally exhausted. So when one twin wanted to do piano lessons, and the other, martial art, I did not know how I was going to make it work.

But as my twins pleaded with me, I reluctantly agreed. How would I add more demanding things to my overstretched schedule? I signed them up, and then it dawned on me that I could wash the clothes that needed ironing on Thursday evenings. Then, I could iron in the night. On Fridays, I could wash the clothes they had worn to school that day, as well as washing their hair and styling it. That would leave Saturdays free. And that was what I did. I felt less tired by dividing my housework over two days.

CHAPTER 10 – TRAVELING OVERSEAS

Traveling through the airports is a headache for everyone. But travelling through the airport with children, is a challenge. And it can be a nightmare for a single mother with twins.

The first time I travelled with my twins alone, through the airport in Florida, was when the babies were about two years old. My sister had agreed to meet me at the airport to sit the twins, while I attended the business meeting.

I had to travel from Bermuda to Florida.

The babies were in their twin stroller, which I tried to maneuver with my right hand. I had a medium sized suitcase that I was pulling with my left hand, a backpack on my back, and the babies' bag over my shoulder. In the babies' bag were expressed breastmilk, breast pump, formula, bottle brush, dishwashing liquid, carrot sauce, diapers, wipes, bottles with distilled water, thermometer, bibs, change of clothes, blankets……

The person who had dropped me off at the airport in Bermuda tried to pull the suitcase, and carry the babies' bag as far as they were allowed inside the airport. From that point, I had to ask the clerk in personnel to help me to Immigration.

While waiting in the Departure Lobby, I deliberately left the twins in their twin stroller for control. They did not like the relatively long wait and started making attempts to escape out of the stroller.

On the airplane, the toddlers would not stay in their seats. They were crying – together like a choir- and were just plain restless. My stress level shot up through the roof. The whole flight was close to a nightmare. I was so relieved when I arrived in Florida to see my sister.

Travel Companion

That was the last time I travelled alone.

For all subsequent business trips, I traveled with someone. I would ask some of my friends in Bermuda, or pay someone to accompany me. They would help me with the suitcases, while I pushed the twin stroller. My stress levels were way lower with another person there.

Also, with someone else there on the trip, I could now take the twins out of their stroller, as there was sufficient people there to supervise and control them.

Check for Ear Infections

According to The National Health Service (UK), "Ear infections are common in babies and small children. They often follow a cold and sometimes cause a temperature."[10]

Whenever my twin daughters had a cold, and it was drawing near for a trip, I would become vigilant for signs of ear infections. I would observe them for fever, pulling on their ears, or just plain irritability. I would also give them their children's Advil and prescription steroid nasal spray, and anti-histamine.

Travel Expenses

It was always very expensive to travel with my twins. As soon as they were two years old, all the airlines started to charge adult airfares for them. While my company would pay for my travel expenses, I would always have to find airfares for my twin daughters,

---

[10] https://www.healthdirect.gov.au/coughs-colds-and-ear-infections-in-children

as well as for the person that was accompanying me. It was very distressing to afford this twice or three times per year, but eventually I had a feel of when I would be required to travel for my business meetings. I started to prepare way in advance as much as was possible. I would ask my manger to inform me way in advance so that I could make the necessary preparations.

I obviously needed car seats and a car when I travelled overseas, because of my toddlers. So I would rent a car and two car seats in advance as well.

This detail planning made the trips more bearable when the time came.

Early Packing

In order for me not to forget anything, I would start packing about a week in advance of my trips. This saved me from last minute packing which caused stress, and also reducing the chance that I would forget anything. Things such as our passports, clothes, thermometers, and diapers were pre-packed. And then I made a list of all the rest of things that had to be packed.

CHAPTER 11 – ASKED FOR HELP

There is no way a single parent of twins can survive on his or her own without some sort of support. I thought I could, and had to. I learned my lesson the hard way.

Help from School

My twin daughters were in pre-school (kindergarten), and I woke up one morning feeling very ill. Nevertheless, I took them to school, as I had no one to call on. I arrived back at home to get myself ready for work, but I had started to feel worse. I had to call in sick to my job. I went from worse to worst throughout the day. And when it was time to collect my twins from school, I could not get up. I called the school's principal and she offered to take my twins home, and to also pick them up the next morning. That day taught me a lesson in asking for help. Since then, I have asked other parents at the twins' school for help when I just cannot manage.

My job can be demanding at times, and sometimes I just cannot change my appointments with clients. If the children's school is having an event that I cannot get to, I ask one of the parents that I am close to, to supervise my twins. I asked a parent just recently to do just that as I could not get out of the appointments for work. The twins' school was having a female luncheon, so I asked a parent to include my daughters at her table for the luncheon. She obliged. I have also collected other parents' children for them, at their requests, if they cannot make it on time when school or afterschool are out.

I surround myself with a few parents in the same class level for clarification in homework and end of school semester tests.

Support from Friends

As a single mother of twins, in a foreign country, with limited money and time, I could not have survived this much, and come this far, without the support of friends both in this country and overseas.

When the twins were only two months old, at the beginning of all the saga, I had to be in court for custody matters frequently. One of my friends offered to sit with the babies in the city, for over two hours in my car, each time, while I went to court for sessions that lasted over two hours. This friend did this over many months as the court case required. I was so touched by her kindness, as she was often on twelve-hour night duty shifts, and would just come straight from work to assist me.

Once I had returned to work, my two months of Legal Aid ended, and I had to retain a private attorney. Because my estranged husband had Legal Aid the entire time, he apparently was in no hurry to conclude the matters in court. In a relatively short time I had incurred a huge legal fee. After venting to two of my friends in Jamaica, I was shocked when they informed me that they had sent me a fairly significant amount of money to help pay towards my legal fees!

Another friend, without my request, decided to 'adopt' the twins. She started sending two parcels of clothes twice a year. I was flabbergasted.

And yet another couple that takes my twins to church from the time they were four years old, to date.

I also had a close circle of friends in Bermuda and overseas, including my family, that kept me sane. They allowed me to cry, curse, and complain for years, on a frequent basis, until my life was normal again.

Called the Police for Support

Friends are central to your life when you are on your own with your children. However, there will be times when you may have to call on other persons in your community for help, and that was what I did.

It was that time that I had told you earlier in this book, of the febrile seizure episode in the evening after 7:00 pm. Twin I was slowly improving as her temperature was coming down. However, we were in the ER until 3:00 am. I did not feel comfortable entering my apartment at that time of the morning with two toddlers, so I called the Police. The Sergeant on duty asked me to repeat my request.

"Sir, I would like the Police to escort me to my apartment, as I have been at the ER until now, and I do not feel comfortable going home at this time of the night with my two toddlers," I said calmly, or perhaps, tiredly.

The Sergeant sent two Police Officers who drove behind my car until I reached my apartment. They then stayed outside until I was safely inside and my lights were out.

CHAPTER 12 – BOUNDARIES

Single parents have to take on the role of the missing parent. The tiredness is palpable on an almost constant basis.

Clinical psychologist Chad Buck stated,

"Boundaries make it possible to allow yourself to recharge. And when you're not totally tapped out, you have more energy to devote to the ones you love. You're also more respectful of their own needs as a result,"

He continued, "If you don't set the limit, then others will set it for you or just ignore that you have limits."[11]

In my case, there was literally no one to hand my twins over to – no parents (both deceased); no siblings (all overseas); and the friends in Bermuda were mostly preoccupied with their own families or work, for those who were here on Work permits.

My Own Time

It has been challenging finding time for myself to refresh and regroup. I tend to work almost at a

---

[11]https://www.huffingtonpost.com/entry/setting-boundaries-benefits_us_57043126e4b0b90ac27088bb

constant rate, on a daily basis. But after I have put my twins to bed, I take a bath and exhale.

Every now and then, one or both twins come in my room with some feeble excuses about 'not feeling well', even though they were just playing ten minutes prior on their tablets, shouting and dancing. Or,

"Mommy you didn't give me a hug."

Or, "I can't sleep."

I have realized that time spent alone, even if it is short time, really revitalizes me. I use this time to return calls, or to talk to my family, surf the Internet, watch a TV show or movie, or just lie there and fantasize how I become so rich that I can finally pay someone to assist me with the twins 24/7.

I promptly send them back to their bedroom, and let them know that this is 'Mommy's time' and that I am exhausted and need some rest. With some protests, they usually leave my room.

Birthdays and Mother's Day

On my twins' birthday, I always make a big ado. On their seventh birthday, I rented a portion of one of the parks; I rented a train; I paid the Bermuda Gombeys to dance; I bought gifts; and their father's relatives got most of the food, decorations, and more gifts. When the twins arrived at their party, they were flabbergasted, flattered, and overwhelmingly happy.

When it is my birthday, or Mother's Day, I treat myself to lunch at a restaurant, or buy myself some gift, or do my nails. I absolutely do no cooking on that day. If the twins ask if they can get a gift too, or if I can cook something special for them, I respond with a resounding 'no'. I explain to them that it is my birthday only, and my time to be focused on. I do not know whether that message has sunken in, but I will continue to reinforce it. I believe that I am teaching my twin daughters that they are important, and so am I, and that it is ok to focus on yourself completely on your special days.

My Own Space

When I was searching for an apartment to rent, shortly after I had left my ex-husband, some of the people I had asked to look out for a place for me, started making suggestions. I had specifically made it known that I was seeking a two-bedroom apartment, and yet people were calling me about one bedroom and studio apartments. In their opinion, it was just me and the girls, so we could all be in the same bed, and the same space.

I insisted that I should have my own bedroom just because I needed my own space. Even when the twins were just a few months old, I had put them in their own bedroom – with a baby monitor.

I believe that boundaries are healthy, in that it makes people value you, and this includes your children. There is mutual respect between you and your children.

When I escape to my own space (bedroom) after putting my twins to their bed, I feel like my physical space is just for me. I can be myself in there.

Boundaries on Myself

I try to put boundaries on my own self, when it comes to the twins. I let them figure things out on their own first, and then I help if they start to struggle.

Recently, the twins brought home their homework. I went about explaining the homework to the point where I began telling them some of the answers. Well, Twin II let me know, in no uncertain terms, that I was not to do their homework for them.

I backed away.

Boundaries on Strangers and Others

I teach my twins to have boundaries for themselves as far as it relates to strangers. I told them that nobody is allowed to touch them or say inappropriate things to them. That they are to tell me whenever anyone tries to touch them inappropriately.

Even when they were just two years old, and we went to the park, they would run up to people that were walking their dogs. Just as my toddlers were getting ready to touch these dogs, I would caution them to always ask the owners' permission first. Apart from perhaps getting bitten by some of these dogs, it was just good manners to ask before touching someone else's property.

CHAPTER 13 – TAKING CARE OF MYSELF

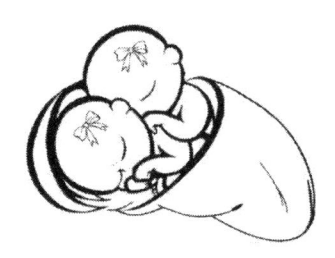

Many parents take good care of their children, at the expense of taking care of themselves. This more pronounced, I believe, in single parents. In many cases, there is no one else there to hand the kids over to, so that you may take a nice bath, or go do your hair, or go to an event. Even though it is hard for couples with children, depending on their availability, they can take turns with the children, so that they can each get a break.

Addressing My Body

I was oblivious to my ill-health for the first four years of my twins' lives. For over two years, I was dealing with a custody battle, and expenses such as daycare fees. And for the next three years, I was paying down my huge legal fees and bank loans, while dealing with anger, sadness, and frustration. I was completely focused on the health and happiness of my twins.

I was talking to a friend that was a member of a gym, and he suggested that I come to check the gym out, as members were given the option of bringing a friend for free for one hour. He had asked his personal trainer to give me a full body worker for the hour that he had paid for himself. I was reluctant to take up the offer, since I did not know how I would be able to afford the gym. My friend said that he had noticed how I had taken most of my commission that I had gotten from my job, to buy bicycles for my twins, and had paid for swimming lessons for their summer camp. Yet, I did not think that I should spend some on myself for my own health.

I was irritated by my friend's comments, but only because they had hit a nerve. He was right.

After the trial session, I used the rest of my commission to pay for a few weeks of gym. I did not know where I would have gotten the money to continue. But the gym owner advised against me stopping, and allowed me to pay him at the end of the month.

The owner of the gym also suggested that my twice a week workout was insufficient to see striking results. But I just did not have any more time in my bursting schedule. I told him that I would have to give two days a week or not come at all.

After a few months, I started to see some changes in my body. I was feeling more confident and beautiful.

I was eating much better – no simple carbs such as white rice, bread, pasta, biscuits. I switched to almond chocolate milk and water. I ate salmon once a week, baked or stewed chicken, fish, nuts, and a lot of steamed or raw vegetables. I started to cook my own food, limiting salt and using olive oil instead of butter.

Within one year, I looked like I had been given a makeover.

Although I am improving, I still struggle with sleeping. As a single mother of twins, one twin is always either sick, being clingy, or trying to push my boundaries of coming into my room. This is where I envy couples who are parents, or people who have support, that are able to sleep in on the weekend.

Addressing My Emotional State

More often than not, a single parent of twins will have some emotional issues. Initially, I came down really hard on myself.

Why did I agree to marry my ex?

How could someone of my consciousness be fooled by my ex?

I was so caught up in how I ended up alone in a foreign country with twins to take care of on my own, that I was becoming bitter with self-beating.

With a lot of encouragement and wisdom from some of my family members and friends, I slowly started to realize that I was poisoning myself. And just like how I started taking care of my body, I made a conscious effort to rectify my emotional state.

That was when I had started the self-talk.

I started to meditate. I asked God to help me to forgive myself and my ex.

My self-confidence and calmness started to improve with time. The children getting older, and more independent, also provided more time for me to focus on myself.

Because I could rarely go out, I got myself a G-box to watch some movies.

My high self-esteem started to rub off on my twins.

Addressing My Spirituality

For every request I had made to God, I entered my answered prayers into a folder. And whenever I doubted anything, I would refer to my over 250 answered prayers.

CHAPTER 14 – FOUGHT FOR MY TWINS

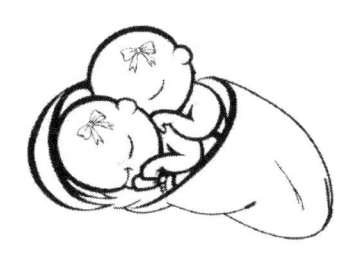

Perhaps some people think that single parents are pushovers and that we are vulnerable, and ready to crumble.

Court Fight

I believe my ex-husband had thought that I could not possibly survive with twin babies in a foreign country with very limited resources. When he decided to launch his harassment campaign through the courts, even though I was exhausted, I fought for my twin daughters.

I did not try at any point, to get back at my ex. I focused on the safety and well-being of my twins. I also insisted that their father spend time with them in a safe environment. Even after he had up and left the island, I told him that I had expected him to contact his daughters, which he tried to do.

Even though my ex had left the island, I had asked the courts to deduct child support from his early retirement pension for the twins. I was in the most expensive country in the world, with a modest salary, and two babies to take care of, as well as myself.

I had to serve my ex in the country to which he had settled in. I had found his address and sent the papers from my attorney to a Bailiff in that country. The signed paper was then sent back by the Bailiff via courier service.

The Supreme Courts finally granted my request and garnished my ex's pension. It was not a lot, but it helped to buy some groceries for a week or two per month.

School Fight

In Bermuda, the children are placed in schools based on their addresses. I had visited the school near to my first apartment, and it was not a good fit for my daughters. Additionally, all of my support group of parents and friends' children were attending another school that was in my zone, but not close to my address.

I had just found another apartment, and this one was closer to my desired school.

I had applied to The Ministry of Education for the desired school, but the reply letter in the mail, had informed me of the undesired school. I immediately called the MOE and told the Administrator that I was appealing their decision. A few weeks later, I was asked to appear before the Appeals Committee. I was very nervous when I walked into the room with a long table of eyes, sizing me up.

I was prepared.

I made all my points – three of them.

They listened attentively. Then one of the committee members asked me,

"So ma'am, you are asking for two spaces?"

"Yes," I calmly answered.

Two weeks later, my twin daughters had gotten two of the three available spaces for my desired school.

Because of the appeals process, my preparedness for school was late, and my twin daughters could only get into different classes. I found this to be very stressful on my twin daughters and myself. On the first day of school, the parents are allowed to escort their children right inside the classes to meet the teachers. I did not know how to split myself. I kept running from one class to the next. One twin had a look of relief when she saw me, but I had to quickly go to the next class to see the other twin.

I just wished their father was there at that moment. I was distressed, and my twins were a bit anxious for their first day of elementary (primary) school.

The rest of the year was also challenging with meeting the teachers, homework, and class birthday parties.

For the next school year, I met with the principal and made a request for my twin daughters to be in the same class, and she granted me my request.

The girls competed with each other, and performed outstandingly well throughout the year. They received several awards for some of their subjects.

The next school year, the principal called and asked whether I had wanted my twin daughters to be placed together again, and I said yes.

Critic Blocking

I try not to criticize my twins and I make sure to fight against those who criticize my children.

My twins are very tall for their height because both their father and I are from tall families. There are people that make comments, even in the presence of my children, in a negative way, of how big they look.

"They are beautiful though, aren't they?"

"Differences make the world more beautiful," are my responses.

Some of them are underhanded and make subtle comments about how they will be good at basketball, to which I tell them, they are super smart, and will be able to do anything they want to do.

I let nothing slip by, and I do not allow my twins to internalize mean comments. I tell them that there is a difference between opinions and facts. I even tell them stories of how I fought back at the bullies and won. I tell them to stand up for themselves.

I behave very self-assured and confident around my children, and I have seen where I have positively influenced their self-confidence.

And speaking of self-confidence, I shower my twin daughters with a lot of daily compliments, every little chance I get. I tell them that they are beautiful; that they are super smart; thoughtful (whenever they do something nice for someone else); and helpful. Positive reinforcement is sometimes much more powerful than criticizing.

I do not care if my twins only have one parent – me. I will always fight for the betterment of my daughters.

CHAPTER 15 – EXTRACURRICULAR ACTIVITIES

I was always tired and still am. Although the girls are more independent, and doing a lot on their own, my accumulated tiredness has come to a head.

When most parents were asking me what extracurricular activities my twins were involved in, I would, unashamedly, say none.

So the question that should be asked is,

"When should your children be enrolled in these extracurricular activities?"

And my simple answer is,

"When you can."

I know what it feels like, when you want your children to do activities on the weekend or after school hours, but you cannot afford the time, or the cost associated with them. Parents have asked me, with slightly raised brows,

"So you don't have your twins in any activities?"

And I would calmly respond,

"No."

I gave no explanation, or made any excuses. I knew I was very tired, and I was not sure if I could continuously afford these activities.

Every summer, I have to find all this money for camps that last for ten weeks in Bermuda. While some parents would say,

"Oh, but this camp is reasonable, it only costs US$200."

My response would be,

"I'm, no. It would cost me US$400 per week.

As I had said earlier, once the twins turned seven years old, they started begging me to enroll them in martial arts class and piano lessons. By this time, my financial situation was starting to improve, so I obliged them.

I have rearranged my housework duties to facilitate the twins' extracurricular activities, because I feel I could do that now.

It's my life and my children, and I will do what I can in order to manage.

CHAPTER 16 – TACKLED BURNOUT

"One in eight parents will struggle with parent burnout. Every parent on the planet knows what it feels like to be a little bit frazzled, frustrated and overwhelmed. That's just normal parenting. When things get into the territory of parent burnout is when things are more prolonged. Everyday feels like a bad day, drifting into a pattern where you feel emotionally disconnected from your child," this, according to the journal, *Frontiers of Psychology*.[12]

I have had many moments when I have felt so overwhelmed with being alone with my twin daughters, especially when they were younger. I knew if I had given in too much, then I would become 'emotionally disconnected'. I was the twins' only parent, so I tried to put in place strategies to help me prevent too much burnout.

The Talk

I have come to realize that young children are able to understand things more than we think. They are very perceptive of so many situations, even when they do not fully grasp every aspect of it.

---

[12]http://www.cbc.ca/news/canada/calgary/parent-burnout-warning-signs-1.4135283

I thought that at five years old, my twins would have some semblance of understanding. So from that age, I have been having 'the talk' with them, about giving their mommy a break. I remind them, when I am beginning to feel overwhelmed, tired, and stressed out, that they only have one parent that has to do everything for them and myself. Somehow, my twins seemed to get it – for the time being at least. Time enough for me to gather myself.

Illness Strategy

Every few months since I have been left on my own, the twins have had some major episodes of the flu, or gastroenteritis. At these times, I have been too tired, or too ill myself, to check on them throughout the night. So I put them in my bed – one on each side of me. That way I could easily assess whether their body temperatures were high, or if they were vomiting.

This action has helped to keep my stress levels down since it made me more tired, if I got up several times every night, during the whole time of their illness.

Discipline Timing

I try not to discipline my twins too much when I am feeling very tired, irritated about something, or just plain angry. Whenever I make the mistake of disciplining them at those times, I tend to overdo it, and that is when I feel guilty and burnt out.

I just tell them to go to their rooms. And I let them know that I am not happy with their behavior. That I cannot speak to them now.

Apparently when I get mad, because they had been acting up, and I am not speaking to them at that moment, it makes them realize that I am not playing around.

I find that just being silent for a while, instead of losing it, has been more effective at controlling my children.

I have also noticed that when I do discipline one of the twins, the other falls in line without me saying anything to her. That has worked every time.

Just Say No

As a single parent of twin girls, I initially felt pressure, from myself at that, to make sure that my twin girls always looked well groomed. I also felt, and especially when they were younger, that I should take them to the park all the time; that I should expose them to as many sports and places as possible. I felt that I should accept every birthday party invitation.

But after a while, as I started to feel exhausted and burnt out, I started to tell my twins 'no'. I only accepted invitations if they fit into my schedules, and I cared little if my twins' hairstyles were not that neat, or their clothes were not that 'cute'.

I felt a sense of relief.

Entertainment

I got myself a G-box so that I could watch some recent movies. This made me feel less sad that I was unable to go see said movies at the movie theater.

Watching a number of movies took my mind off myself, for the time I was watching them, and this helped me to relax.

Dancing

Twice a year, one of my friends would come and sit my twins so that I could go dancing.

I love to dance, and if I may say, I am good at it. I would dance for three hours non-stop, on the dance floor. I feel so happy when I am dancing. Many days after I had gone dancing, I would still be in a state of euphoria.

CHAPTER 16 – DEALING WITH TWIN COMPETITIVENESS

When you have a two-parent family home, many times, the attention demanded by the children can be shared between the two parents. This is clearly not the case with single parents of twins.

I have noticed, that since the death of their father, when they were six years old, that the twins have been quite clingy to me. Additionally, the sibling rivalry between them is striking.

So they have begun to 'fight' for my attention more. If I should give Twin I a compliment, telling her that she was so beautiful. Twin II would immediately start asking if she was beautiful too. Or one would tell me that I preferred the other.

This would stress me somewhat, as it was becoming more frequent, and I was worried that I was not giving them enough individual attention. My ideal situation would have been to leave one twin at home, and have a full Twin I day, and then alternate with Twin II the other.

But my life is not ideal. Single parents' lives are far from that.

Fairness

I endeavor to not come across to my twin girls as biased towards anyone of them. I give them compliments, attention, discipline, and have similar expectations of them. There is no preferential treatment to any of them.

At bedtime, the twins like it when I lay down beside them in their beds. I use the clock to time the time I spend with both. That way the other twin cannot say that I had given more time to the other twin, unless of course, one twin is ill or is having nightmares. Sometimes, while lying in one twin's bed, the other twin tries to insert herself in the twin's time while I'm on her bed. I always insist that she waits her turn. I completely focus on the twin that I am lying beside. She gets to tell me everything about her day, or play any game with me that she desires, or I tell her a story.

Then I do the same for the other twin – rinse and repeat.

Taking Turns

All children are taught to take turns. It is a part of being social, and it creates harmony and order.

My twins, as toddlers, did not want to take turns. Human nature can be set on the selfish default. So I have been teaching my twins to take turns in speaking to each other and to me. Taking turns to play, or for me to help them with their homework, or for using my bedroom during the daytime.

It is still a struggle, but they are slowly learning.

Two Different Persons

Because my twin daughters are identical, people have been asking me the same question from the time that the twins were toddlers,

"Do they have the same personality?"

Initially, after I was on my own, and very stressed, it was easy to treat my twins as one person split in two. But the twins would not have it for long. They soon made me know that they were two different persons.

Twin I's personality, by the age of three years old, started to emerge as a little shy, yet very sociable, just like me. She is very thoughtful and caring, and talks incessantly. She has always been the bigger twin, even in utero, and at birth. She is slightly taller than Twin II. She tends to take calculated risks.

Twin II is a bit more conservative, and is very discriminating when it comes to her friend choices. She knows what she wants and makes it known. Surprisingly, she is somewhat of a daredevil. She is feisty and stands up for herself, just like me. She is quieter and has the ability to focus way longer than Twin I can.

See? Two different personalities.

It is amazing to see how my personality has been shared over two different persons. If you want to know how you act, just take a look at your children. Some of it will be embarrassing, and some fantastic.

I try to support their differences, although I still try to force them to dress alike. This is evident at meal times, and what I pack for their school lunches. I will not force one twin to eat what the other is eating. I've sometimes used reverse psychology to make the twins appear to be choosing their meals. I would give them two options only, from which to choose. That option makes them feel important, as if they are in charge of their lives. It works every time.

Commonalities

While the twins have their own strikingly different personalities, they do have some things in common.

They are both very smart girls. They have been showing their brilliance since they were in kindergarten school. Since their time in elementary (primary) school, their performance has been even more outstanding.

They are both very determined. Every year they say they what they want for Christmas, and I tell them to save their own money, because their desired gifts are too expensive. So they do chores for US$2 or $5.

They save money that other people give them for their birthdays, or they get funds from relatives. They are so fulfilled and confident every time that they are buying their gifts that I thought were too expensive to get.

My twin daughters love each other, but they fight sometimes too. They fought in my womb, I guess for more space. Whenever one of the twins was not so nice to the other, and I tried to discipline the 'perpetrator', the 'victim' twin would scold me! Imagine that. I consider that 'ganging' up on me.

As newborn babies, they would sleep on top of each other, when they were placed together in the same crib or playpen. As toddlers, they would hold hands while walking. They used to light up my heart, as I watched them play 'hide and seek' behind the curtains in the living room. They seem to understand each other deeply, as one twin can usually explain, in detail, what the other twin is trying to say.

CHAPTER 17 – FINAL ANALYSIS

I have shared all my core strategies for literally raising my twins on my own. No parent has it easy, unless they have given up their child to be fully raised by another. But it is even more challenging when you are a single parent, raising children that are at the exact stage of development, needs, and dependence.

But to say that it is mostly a challenge is just a part of it. There are positive spinoffs for being a single parent, especially of twins:

- You're creating two persons that are manifesting different aspects of your personality. You are looking at two clones of yourself, if you will. You get to fully re-assess yourself, should you see any behavior in your children that you are not proud of.
- All your efforts from the time you have been left to raise your twins alone, will certainly pay off in some way, and will be accredited to only you. No one else will be able to say that it was because of their contributions.
- The greatest benefit of being a single parent of twins is that you will become so strong that you may not recognize yourself anymore. My resilience was being built from the time I had to bottle and breastfeed my twin daughters simultaneously, alone; potty train them on my own; do homework and reviews for exams often; take them to all the necessary

functions, and school, even when I was sick. I have the fortitude to continue to raise my twins, even while inspiring others. That if I can do it, then they definitely can too.

- You will have two people in the world that thinks the world of you, and love you - times two.

You'll be great at whatever you put your mind to.

-Marcella Evans

Printed in Great Britain
by Amazon